Reducing Waste

Andrew Einspruch

Smart Apple Media
P.O. Box 3263
Mankato, MN, 56002

First published in 2010 by
MACMILLAN EDUCATION AUSTRALIA PTY LTD
15–19 Claremont St, South Yarra, Australia 3141

Visit our web site at www.macmillan.com.au or go directly to www.macmillanlibrary.com.au

Associated companies and representatives throughout the world.

Library of Congress Cataloging-in-Publication Data

Einspruch, Andrew.
    Reducing waste / Andrew Einspruch.
       p. cm. — (Living sustainably)
    Includes index.
    ISBN 978-1-59920-553-3 (library binding)
    1. Waste minimization—Juvenile literature. 2. Refuse and refuse disposal—Juvenile literature. I. Title.
    TD793.9.E365 2011
    363.72'8—dc22
                              2009045099

Publisher: Carmel Heron   Designer: Kerri Wilson (cover and text)
Managing Editor: Vanessa Lanaway   Page layout: Kerri Wilson
Editor: Laura Jeanne Gobal   Photo Researcher: Jes Senbergs (management: Debbie Gallagher)
Proofreader: Helena Newton   Production Controller: Vanessa Johnson

Manufactured in China by Macmillan Production (Asia) Ltd.
Kwun Tong, Kowloon, Hong Kong
Supplier Code: CP January 2010

Acknowledgments

The author and the publisher are grateful to the following for permission to reproduce copyright material:

Front cover photograph of girl recycling cans, courtesy of Photolibrary/Jupiterimages.

Photographs courtesy of © Lynda Richardson/Corbis, 10; © Ariel Skelley/Corbis, 16; Rob Cruse, 19; Steven Alvarez/Getty Images, 30; Andreas Pollok/Getty Images, 18; Mark Segal/Getty Images, 29; Peter Ziminski/Getty Images, 4; © Monika Adamczyk/iStockphoto, 21; © Carmen Martinez/iStockphoto, 15; © Chris Price/iStockphoto, 22; © Ralph 125/iStockphoto, 11; © Courtney Weittenhiller/ iStockphoto, 26; © Ivonne Wierink van Wetten/iStockphoto, 17; © Yin Yang/iStockphoto, 7; Jupiter Images, 20; MEA, 24; Newspix/ News Ltd/Melissa di Padova, 28; Patagonia, 27; Photolibrary © Vicki Beaver/Alamy, 14; Photolibrary © Ianni Dimitrov/Alamy, 5; Photolibrary © Steven May/Alamy, 3, 6; Photolibrary © Alex Segre/Alamy, 9; Photolibrary © UrbanZone/Alamy, 13; Photolibrary/ Francesca Yorke, 23; Shutterstock, 12, 25 (left); © Pavel Drozda/Shutterstock, 25 (top); © MdN/Shutterstock, 25 (bottom).

While every care has been taken to trace and acknowledge copyright, the publisher tenders their apologies for any accidental infringement where copyright has proved untraceable. Where the attempt has been unsuccessful, the publisher welcomes information that would redress the situation.

Contents

When a word is printed in **bold**, you can look up
its meaning in the Glossary on page 31.

Living Sustainably

Living sustainably means using things carefully so there is enough left for people in the future. To live sustainably, we need to look after Earth and its **resources**.

If we cut down too many trees now, there will not be enough wood in the future.

The things we do make a difference. We can use water, energy, and other resources wisely. Reducing waste is one way we can help make a sustainable world.

We can reduce waste by carrying groceries in a bag that can be used again.

Reducing Waste

Earth's resources are used to make things, such as pizza boxes, plastic bags, and toys. When we throw these things away, they become waste.

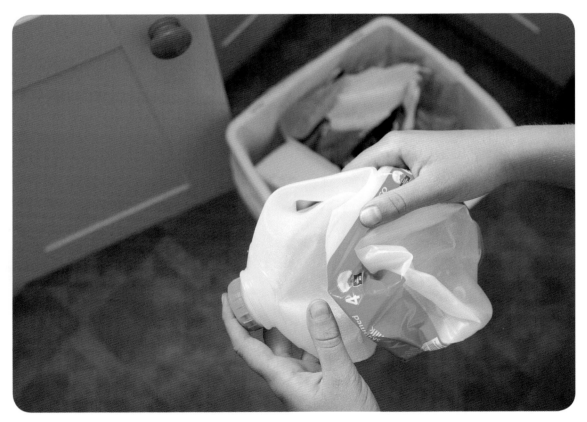

Plastic bottles are often thrown away as waste.

A lot of waste is created around the world every year. Some countries create more waste than others.

The world's top 10 creators of waste

Rank	Country	Amount of waste per person, per year
1	United States	1,676 pounds (760 kg)
2	Australia	1,521 pounds (690 kg)
3	Denmark	1,455 pounds (660 kg)
4	Switzerland	1,433 pounds (650 kg)
5	Canada	1,411 pounds (640 kg)
6	Norway	1,367 pounds (620 kg)
7	Netherlands	1,345 pounds (610 kg)
8	Austria	1,235 pounds (560 kg)
9	United Kingdom	1,235 pounds (560 kg)
10	Ireland	1,235 pounds (560 kg)

What Is in Waste?

There are many things in waste. Garden waste, such as lawn clippings, makes up most of the waste from a home.

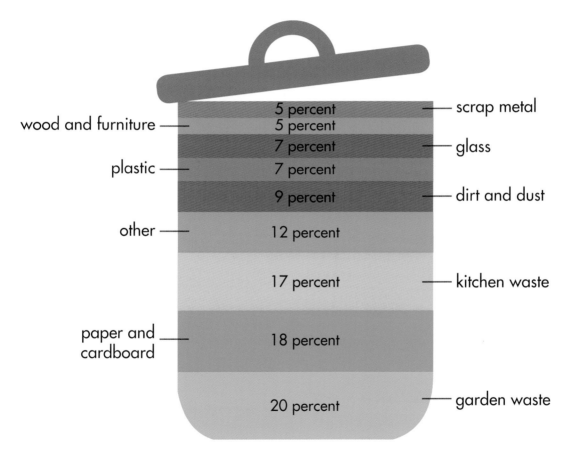

wood and furniture	5 percent — scrap metal
	5 percent
	7 percent — glass
plastic	7 percent
	9 percent — dirt and dust
other	12 percent
	17 percent — kitchen waste
paper and cardboard	18 percent
	20 percent — garden waste

This diagram shows the different types of waste thrown away by a household.

Many things that become waste are used only for a short time. Containers and wrappers that hold food are thrown away almost immediately. That is a real waste!

Fast-food containers are used for only a short time before they become waste.

What Happens to Waste?

Most waste is placed in a big hole in the ground and covered with soil. This is called a landfill. Buried waste in landfills can take many years to **decompose**.

Landfills take up a lot of space and get full very quickly.

Waste can also be thrown into a dump. Waste in dumps lies uncovered. Both landfills and dumps are a type of **pollution**. They are harmful to the **environment**.

When waste decomposes in landfills and dumps, it releases gases that harm the environment.

Reduce, Reuse, Recycle

There are three rules to follow when dealing with waste: reduce, reuse, and recycle. Understanding these rules can help us make better choices. Better choices will lead to sustainable living.

When we see this sign, we are reminded to make better choices.

Reduce

Reducing waste means creating less waste. If we create less waste, landfills and dumps will not fill up so quickly.

The best way to reduce waste is to avoid buying things we do not need.

Reuse

To reuse means to use something again instead of throwing it away. We can reuse something ourselves or give it to someone else so they can use it.

Old clothes can be given to stores that resell them so that other people can use them.

Recycle

To recycle means to make something new out of something that has already been used. There are many things that can be recycled, including paper, glass, and some plastic.

To recycle paper, glass, or plastic, place it in the correct recycling bin.

Reduce Waste when Eating

We can reduce waste by cooking with fresh ingredients instead of canned ingredients. Cooking also creates less **packaging** than takeout or food that has already been prepared.

Making soup with fresh tomatoes creates less waste than using canned tomatoes or eating canned soup.

A Waste-free Lunch

Try bringing a waste-free lunch to school so nothing ends up in the trash. Use napkins, containers, forks, and spoons that can be washed and reused.

It is important to pack the right amount of food so that nothing is wasted.

Reduce Waste by Repairing

We can reduce waste by repairing things that are broken instead of replacing them. Toys, televisions, and many other things can usually be repaired when something is wrong.

Repairing toys instead of throwing them away is one way to reduce waste.

Repairing things helps reduce waste.
- Painting is an easy way to make some things look new again.
- Torn clothes can be sewn back together and buttons can be sewn back on.

Painting outdoor furniture can protect it from the weather and help it last longer.

Reduce Waste by Sharing, Swapping, and Making

Sharing things reduces waste. When we share something, more people get to use the shared item. This means fewer people have to buy their own and less waste is created.

Books, toys, and movies are all things that can be shared to help reduce waste.

Swapping and making things can also reduce waste. We can swap things we do not want with friends. We can also make cards and presents instead of buying them.

Making cards and presents is fun and reduces waste.

Reduce Waste with Worm Farms and Compost

Using a worm farm or making **compost** means kitchen scraps and garden waste stay out of the garbage. In worm farms, worms eat the kitchen scraps.

Keeping a worm farm or compost bin at home is an easy way to reduce waste.

In a compost bin, kitchen scraps and garden waste decompose naturally. The remains from worm farms and compost bins can be used in a garden.

The remains from worm farms and compost bins help plants grow well.

Reuse Containers by Refilling

We can also reduce waste by reusing containers that can be refilled. For example, we can buy refills of laundry detergent instead of new bottles.

Buying refills of laundry detergent and fabric softener reduce waste because no new bottles are bought.

Other things that can be refilled include:
- mechanical pencils
- food containers
- drink bottles

Making the right choice when buying pencils, food containers, and drink bottles helps reduce waste.

Recycling

Most communities have recycling programs. The people who run these programs collect waste that can be recycled. This includes paper, glass, and plastic. Recycling helps reduce waste.

Some communities collect recyclable items from homes in special containers.

Recyclable items can be made into interesting things. For example, plastic bottles can be recycled into shirts, fences, packaging material, and compost bins.

This sweater is made from recycled plastic bottles.

Share the Message

Reducing waste is an important message to share with your friends. Ask your teacher if your class can make posters about reducing waste to put up around the school.

Share the message about reducing waste with fun posters.

A Waste-smart School

Stowe Elementary School in Minnesota is a **waste-smart** school. Students recycle many different things and have reduced the school's food waste.

Students at this school sort their waste and place it in different recycling bins.

A Sustainable World

Reducing waste is one way to live sustainably. How many ways can you reduce waste today? Your choices and actions will help make a sustainable world.

Make a list of the things you can do every day to reduce waste.